Royal Doulton

Limited
LOVING-CUPS
AND JUGS

RICHARD DENNIS
144 KENSINGTON CHURCH STREET
LONDON W8 4BN
Tel 01–727 2061

Foreword

I am very grateful to Royal Doulton Tableware Limited for their assistance in producing this booklet and would like to acknowledge my debt to Desmond Eyles for his research into Doulton records and to thank Mr and Mrs Robert Fortune for their kind co-operation. We have illustrated both sides of the 30 loving-cups and jugs that form this series, a highly collectable group, which includes three which were not produced as Limited Editions but were made in similar, small quantities, and the 'Jackdaw of Rheims', a trial jug never put into production. The signatures are not always constant as their clarity depends on the moulding and glazing. As always, we are keen to hear of variations and hopefully of unrecorded trial jugs. I am sure it is the wish of collectors that the historical tradition of the series be continued by Royal Doulton.

RICHARD DENNIS

Each limited edition jug and loving-cup was accompanied by a numbered ornamental certificate. This is the one issued with the Three Musketeers loving-cup.

Introduction

The Limited Edition presentation pieces, emblazoned with vigorously modelled popular subjects, are yet another instance of the creative talents of Charles J. Noke, Royal Doulton's former Art Director. In his fertile mind the concept of Series Ware was developed, closely followed by the prolific figure and character jug collections and in between times, during the 1930s, he masterminded the Limited Edition range.

Modelling was Noke's particular interest and when he was not occupied with his many administrative responsibilities, he was to be found in his studio manipulating his latest ideas in clay. One of his former students, Reginald Johnson, recalls him at work in the late 1920s on the germ of an idea for prestige pieces decorated with bas relief scenes. Noke was no doubt influenced by earlier Staffordshire traditions, as he had been before in the evolution of his figure and character jug designs. Perhaps in the case of the Limited Edition ware he was looking at the popular slip cast relief jugs which were produced at many factories in the Stoke area in the Victorian period. These, like Noke's successors, served primarily as ornaments and reflected all the contemporary tastes in subject matter.

Assisting Noke in the development of this new style was his most accomplished assistant, Harry Fenton. His signature is to be found alongside Noke's on many of the Limited Edition items but it is not quite clear what the division of labour was. Certainly with these wares it was not just a case of Noke, as Art Director, stamping his seal of approval. For instance, Prince George is known to have admired the Dickens Jug that Noke was personally modelling during the Royal Visit to the pottery in 1931, and the unfinished jug is subsequently illustrated in the Pottery Gazette of the same year.

By 1930 the first essay in this new genre was being marketed – 'The Master of Foxhounds Presentation Jug.' The main characteristics of the Limited Edition series are all displayed in this early piece. Forceful, animated modelling in low relief encompasses the vessel which is painted in rich glowing colours underglaze. William Grace, one of Doulton's longest serving artists, specialised in the painting of these slip-cast wares, the last one by his hand being the 1953 Coronation cup.

The lip and handle of the presentation jugs often continue the decorative theme in a novel way. In the case of the MFH jug (as the first jug is commonly known) the lip is in the form of a rooster's head, whilst the handle is a whip. Other bizarre appendages include animal heads and coconut palm handles. It is interesting to note that this amusing concept is later adopted in the character jug range although this is hardly surprising as Noke and Fenton pioneered this collection too.

The MFH jug was quickly followed the next year by 'The Regency Coach Jug' and thereafter each successive year saw the introduction of several new titles. Noke's predilection for the literary classics obviously influenced the choice of subject matter for many of these prestige pieces. The personalities of over fifty Dickens characters are superbly captured by Noke in a fitting tribute to his hero, aptly entitled the 'Dickens Dream Jug', whilst on the 'Shakespeare Jug' some of the bard's best-known characters form a triumphal procession round the vessel.

As well as personalities, noted incidents from famous adventure stories or poems are also rendered in relief. Stevenson's Long John Silver searches for the hidden booty on the 'Treasure Island Jug' and the unfortunate children of Hamelin are lured away in Noke's interpretation of the 'Pied Piper'.

Folk heroes, be they real or fictitious, are inevitably colourful characters and thus eminently suitable as subject matter for these lively jugs. 'Robin Hood' is portrayed with his Merry Men, 'Guy Fawkes' is surprised in the act of trying to blow up the Houses of Parliament and, of course, the exploits of our seafaring heroes, Drake, Nelson and Cook are duly romanticised.

Whilst these jugs celebrate actual events, strictly speaking they do not fall into the commemorative category as their years of issue rarely coincide with any special dates. In fact, in most of the presentation jug range, there appears to be no logical progression in the choice of subject and the date they were introduced. However, Noke realised, at an early stage, the potential of these imposing jugs as vehicles to commemorate political and royal events.

The bicentenary of the birth of George Washington was marked in 1932 by a truly patriotic jug complete with stars and stripes, made exclusively for the American market. In 1938 the 'Captain Philip Jug' commemorated the one hundred and fiftieth anniversary of the founding of the Colony of New South Wales.

There was no shortage of royal events to celebrate during the 1930s with the Silver Jubilee of George V and Queen Mary, the Coronation of Edward VIII and the Coronation of George VI and Queen Elizabeth. The pomp and circumstance of all these occasions is effectively recorded on a selection of presentation jugs and loving-cups in various sizes. The format of the royal portrait amidst flags and heraldic devices set a precedent for royal commemoratives long after Charles Noke's death in 1941. His son Cecil continued the tradition when designing the loving-cup for the Coronation of Queen Elizabeth II in 1953. In more recent years, Reginald Johnson, now a consultant designer to Royal Doulton and formerly a student of Noke Senior, has revived the richly-coloured format for the Silver Jubilee celebrations of 1977.

This latest piece was issued in a limited edition of 250 but the run of previous editions varied, up to a maximum of 2,000 pieces, the exceptions being the 'Dickens Dream Jug' and the 'Wordsworth Jug' which appear to have been unlimited.

It is known that the proposed edition of the George Washington Jug was never completed as it became obvious at an early stage that it was not going to fulfil sales expectations. This, accompanied by the fact that it was only sold in America, makes it one of the rarest jugs today.

It might be expected also that the abdication of Edward VIII would cause his coronation commemoratives to be amongst the rarer pieces as only 1,080 large loving-cups and 454 small had been produced and sold by the time he made his announcement. However, strangely enough they turn up as frequently as those made to commemorate his brother's coronation.

So far three unrecorded jugs have come to light recently – the striking 'Jackdaw of Rheims Jug'. Possibly there are other examples around of this experimental nature, but so far there is no evidence that this particular jug ever went into production. Trials of two other jugs were also made, 'I. T. Wigg, Broom-man,' and 'Roger Solemel, Cobbler.'

Each limited edition jug or loving-cup was numbered on the base and accompanied by a certificate of authenticity, usually a very elaborate document. The base of the jug could be equally decorative, incorporating, in some cases, a commemorative inscription of lines from the poem represented. Perhaps the most novel treatment of a base is on the 'Treasure Island Jug' which illustrates the treasure chart.

It is this attention to detail and overall presentation which enhances this range of prestige jugs and, together with skilfully modelled decoration and rich colour schemes, makes them so admired amongst collectors today. No doubt many would envy the 1930s customer who could buy these jugs for around £3 or even the 1950s collector who could have bought the Coronation cup for £10 approximately, particularly as this field of collecting gains in popularity and prices inflate accordingly.

LOUISE IRVINE
Director, Royal Doulton
International Collectors' Club

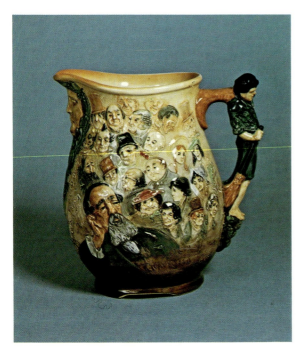

Dickens Dream Jug

Edition: unlimited but
probably about 1,000
Date issued: 1933
Height: 10½ in
Signed: NOKE

Although not a limited edition this jug is clearly of the category and illustrates the outstanding popularity of Charles Dickens with both Noke and the public which led to the production of a jug for general sale. The following characters are depicted in relief:
BARNABY RUDGE – Barnaby Rudge, Mr Varden
BLEAK HOUSE – Chadband, Poor Jo
THE CHIMES – Trotty Veck
A CHRISTMAS CAROL – Little Tim, Bob Cratchett
DAVID COPPERFIELD – David Copperfield, Old Pegotty, Little Emily, Dora, Micawber, Uriah Heep, Betsy Trotwood, Barkis, Mr Copperfield, Mr Dick, Steerforth
DOMBEY & SON – Captain Cuttle, Mr Dombey, Mr Carker, Mr Toots
MARK TAPLEY – Mark Tapley
MARTIN CHUZZLEWIT – Martin Chuzzlewit, Tom Pinch, Pecksniff, Sairey Gamp, Poll Sweedlepipe
NICHOLAS NICKLEBY – Kate Nickleby, Squeers, Mantalini
OLD CURIOSITY SHOP – Sampson Brass, Little Nell, Nell's Grandfather, the Marchioness
OLIVER TWIST – Bill Sykes, Bumble, Fagin, Artful Dodger
THE PICKWICK PAPERS – Mr Pickwick, Mrs Bardell, Mr Winkle, Sam Weller, Stiggins, Fat Boy, Bob Sawyer, Serjeant Buzfuz, Tracy Tupman, Jingle, two of the Pickwick Club.

The handle is modelled as Poor Jo, the crossing-sweeper, Dickens is portrayed on the side with the inscription 'Keep my memory Green' and all the characters illustrated are listed on the base.

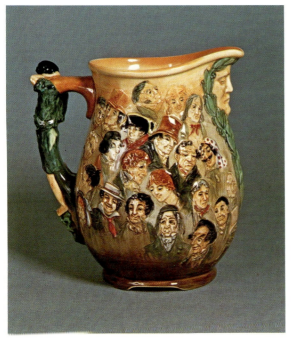

Charles Dickens Jug

Limited edition of 1,000
Date issued: 1936
Height: 10½ in
Signed: NOKE & H FENTON

Charles Dickens (1812–71) received little education as his father was jailed for debt while he was a boy but despite this he began reporting Parliamentary debates for the 'Morning Chronicle' in 1835 and contributed sketches of everyday life to various periodicals. His first novel, 'The Posthumous Papers of the Pickwick Club', originally appeared in 20 monthly issues before publication in book form. In 1842 he visited the USA where he became an abolitionist and gleaned background information for 'Martin Chuzzlewit'. His sudden death was deeply felt as his detailed and accurate accounts of life in Victorian England were universally appreciated.

The jug features some of his most popular characters: Sam Weller cleaning boots; the Artful Dodger picking Barnaby Rudge's pocket, with Mr Micawber in the background and Little Nell in front; Bill Sykes and his dog; Bumble and Tony Weller; Poor Jo, Fagin and Sairey Gamp with Dick Swiveller, Serjeant Buzfuz and Mrs Bardell behind; Pecksniff; Sydney Carton; Pickwick; Mantalini and Fat Boy with Trotty Veck behind. These figures are very similar to those on the Series Ware which were based on the designs of Joseph Clayton Clark or 'Kyd'. Below the rim is a continuous coaching scene, the lip is a mask of Dickens' head and the handle shows an open book inscribed 'DICKENS MASTER OF SMILES AND TEARS'. In raised letters above the base is 'LORD KEEP MY MEMORY GREEN'.

Admiral Lord Nelson Loving-Cup

Limited edition of 600
Date issued: 1935
Height: 10½ in
Signed: NOKE & FENTON

Horatio Nelson (1758–1805) was born at Burnham-Thorpe, Norfolk, and while still a boy joined the navy as a midshipman in his uncle's ship. He proceeded to work his way up through the ranks, promotion being rapid during the war against the French. Nelson suffered two disabilities, losing an eye off Calvi, Corsica, in 1794 and an arm at Santa Cruz in 1797, but this did not prevent him continuing his outstanding career, and at times he even took advantage of his handicaps: during the Battle of Copenhagen he put the telescope to his blind eye and, truthfully saying he could not see a signal to disengage from battle, won a famous victory. At Trafalgar he sought to inspire the fleet with his signal 'England expects that every man will do his duty' and sailed toward the French playing 'Heart of Oak' and 'Rule Britannia'. Fatally wounded, his last words 'Thank God I have done my Duty' well illustrate the courage and dedication of this extraordinary man.

The loving-cup, with its block and tackle handles, shows scenes from the Battle of Trafalgar: Nelson on board his flagship 'Victory', with ENGLAND EXPECTS incised underneath, and a longboat rescuing sailors from the sea before two ships engaged in battle, with IT WAS IN TRAFALGAR BAY incised below.

Sir Francis Drake Jug

Limited edition of 500
Date issued: 1933
Height: 10½ in
Signed: NOKE & FENTON

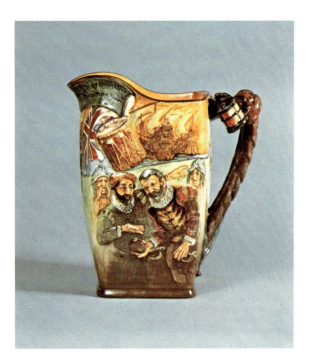

Sir Francis Drake is undoubtedly the most famous of those Elizabethans who, through their seamanship and courage, made England a great sea power. In 1577 he led an expedition around the world, his backers including Queen Elizabeth I, the Earl of Leicester, Hatton, Walsingham, Hawkins and the two Wynters. He returned in the 'Golden Hind' with a hold full of treasure and was knighted on the ship's deck. His other exploits included 'singeing the King of Spain's beard' by burning the Spanish fleet at Cadiz and sailing as Vice-Admiral against the Armada. According to tradition he insisted on finishing his game of bowls when the Armada was sighted, saying 'There is plenty of time to win this game and thrash the Spaniards too.'

The jug with its rope handle complete with ship's lantern records two of these events: Drake with the Queen and other backers before the 'Golden Hind', and playing bowls on Plymouth Hoe while awaiting the Armada. An ornate drum is also shown – there is a legend that when England is threatened Drake can be recalled by beating this drum, and under the lip is part of 'Drake's Drum' by Sir Henry Newbolt: 'Take my drum to England, hang it by the shore. Strike it when your powder's runnin' low'. It continues 'If the Dons sight Devon, I'll quit the port o' heaven An' drum them up the Channel as we drummed them long ago.'

Jan Van Riebeeck Loving-Cup

Limited edition of 300
Date issued: c.1935
Height: 10¼ in
Signed: NOKE & FENTON

With the growth of the spice trade the Dutch East India Company decided in 1648 to establish a foothold at the Cape of Good Hope and chose as commander a young ship's surgeon, Jan Van Riebeeck. On Christmas Eve 1651 he set sail with his wife and son on the 'Dromedarius' accompanied by two support ships, dropping anchor below Table Mountain on April 6th 1652. Van Riebeeck, a resolute and energetic man, was ordered to build a fort and provide fresh water, vegetables and meat to passing ships. To prevent contact with the natives he built a hedge of bitter-almonds around the settlement, the remains of which can still be seen. When he left ten years later, the base was well established and a small group of settlers had been given permission to start farming the land for themselves.

The loving-cup shows the first settlers rowing to shore from the ships, which are anchored below Table Mountain. On the reverse Jan Van Riebeeck is praying before the Dutch national flag at the Cape. The handles are modelled as full-length figures of Van Riebeeck, and on the base is 'Landing at the Cape of Good Hope 1652. The achievement of this mission marked the beginning of the great Dominion which is now the Union of South Africa'.

George Washington Bicentenary Jug

Limited edition of 1,000 but run never completed
Date issued: 1932
Height: 10¾ in
Signed: NOKE & H FENTON

George Washington (1732–99) began his military career as aide-de-camp to General Braddock in the last French and Indian wars, emerging as a full colonel, before returning to farm his Virginian estate. He remained on his lands for the next 15 years until the worsening crisis with Britain led to his becoming a delegate to the First Continental Congress in Philadelphia. Within a year he was Commander-in-Chief of the Army of the United Colonies (1775) leading the war effort which culminated in the surrender of Cornwallis in Yorktown in 1781. He was elected first President of the United States in 1789 and returned for a second term before retiring from politics.

The jug, with its handle of the Stars and Stripes, features a mask of Washington's head modelled as the lip, with a list of the signatories to the Declaration of Independence, headed by John Hancock, below. On one side Washington stands, in military uniform, with fellow officers while on the other he is in civil dress in front of the Capitol. Below these scenes are respectively 'FIRST IN PEACE FIRST IN WAR' and 'First in the hearts of his countrymen', a quotation from a speech given by Henry Lee in the House of Representatives in 1799. Around the bottom runs 'DECLARATION OF INDEPENDENCE'.

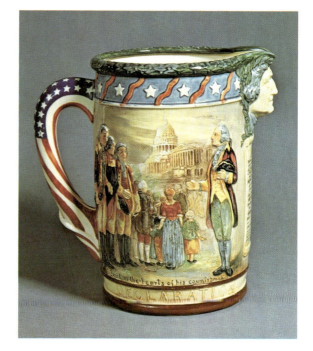

Captain Phillip Jug

Limited edition of 350
Date issued: 1938
Height: 9¼ in
Signed: NOKE & H FENTON

Arthur Phillip (1738–1814) entered the navy as a midshipman in 1755, and by the time he was selected to found the first penal colony in New South Wales (1786) had reached the rank of Post Captain with a good though undistinguished record. He was, however, known as a determined and incorruptible man and during his tenure showed surprising vision. It took eight months for this first fleet of eleven ships to reach Botany Bay in 1788 where the convicts who were to form the workforce of the settlement of Sydney were formally transferred to Captain Phillip. As Governor he had wide powers to appoint Justices, officers, ministers, levy armed forces, execute martial law and grant lands but was handicapped by the time it took for fresh suppplies and communications to arrive from England. His command was short-lived but by the time he left in 1792 there were 86 free settlers to farm the land including ex-convicts and marines.

The jug depicts the flagship 'Sirius' sailing to Australia and Captain Phillip with his officers on shore toasting the flag. The lip is modelled as a mask of his head, with around the bottom the words 'COLONY NEW SOUTH WALES FOUNDED JANUARY 1788 SYDNEY'. A band of eucalyptus leaves adorns the rim while underneath the handle is a list of the governors from Phillip to Wakehurst in 1938.

Captain Cook Loving-Cup

Limited edition of 350
Date issued: 1933
Height: $9\frac{1}{2}$ in
Signed: NOKE & FENTON

Captain James Cook (1728–79) was born in Yorkshire and joined the navy as an able-seaman in 1755. He worked his way up through the ranks by natural ability and became a skilled cartographer and competent navigator. On board the 'Endeavour' he led the 1768–71 expedition to observe the transit of Venus, then sailed south and west to circumnavigate New Zealand, proving it was composed of two islands. Cook then crossed the Tasman Sea to become the first man to see the East Coast of Australia, which he accurately charted. Landing in Botany Bay he took possession of half the continent in the name of the Crown. On his next voyage he explored the South Pacific, following this with an attempt to discover a passage from the North Pacific to the Atlantic during which he was killed by natives on Hawaii.

The loving-cup commemorates Cook's landing at Botany Bay: on one side a party of crewmen are stepping ashore from a longboat, on the other Cook surveys the interior accompanied by his officers. The handles take the form of coconut palms.

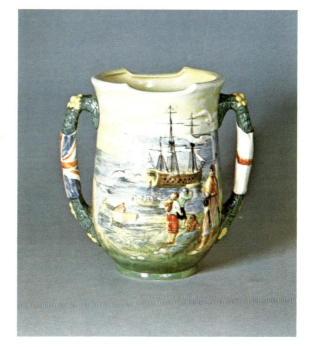

The Village Blacksmith Jug

Limited edition of 600
Date issued: 1936
Height: 7¾ in
Signed: NOKE

Henry Wadsworth Longfellow (1807–82) was born in Portland, Maine, USA. He became a professor of modern languages at Harvard and travelled extensively in Europe, being the guest of Dickens in 1842.

Most of his writing was romantic prose and 'The Village Blacksmith' idealises the image of the hard-working smithy at toil in a sleepy village. Two verses in particular are well illustrated on the jug:

Under a spreading chestnut tree
The village smithy stands;
The smith, a mighty man is he,
With large and sinewy hands;
And the muscles of his brawny arms
Are strong as iron bands

And the children coming home from school
look in the open door
They love to see the flaming forge,
And hear the bellows roar,
And catch the burning sparks that fly
Like chaff from a threshing floor

Featured on the base of the handle is a milestone with the poem's title on one side and LONG-FELLOW 1842 on the reverse, the date of the poem's publication in 'Ballads and other poems'.

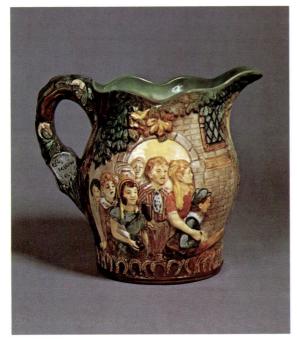

John Peel Loving-Cup

Limited edition of 500
Date issued: 1933
Height: 9 in
Unsigned

John Peel (1776–1854) was born in Caldeck, Cumberland, and became well known as master of his own pack of hounds, named after him. The famous hunting-song 'D'ye ken John Peel' was written over a drink by John Woodcock Graves after the funeral of a mutual friend, to the tune of 'Bonnie Annie', the regimental march of the Border Regiment. The song mentions some of the hounds by name: Ruby, Ranter, Ringwood, Bellman and True, while the final verse, composed after John Peel's death states that he lived at Troutbeck.

D'ye ken John Peel with his coat so gay?
D'ye ken John Peel at the break of the day?
D'ye ken John Peel when he's far, far away,
With his hounds and his horn in the morning?
For the sound of his horn brought me from
  my bed,
And the cry of his hounds which he oft-times
  led,
Peel's view-halloo would awaken the dead,
Or the fox from his lair in the morning.

The handles of the loving-cup are beautifully modelled as foxes heads above riding whips, with on one side John Peel in his hunting pink, accompanied by his friends and favourite hounds, with 'D'ye ken John Peel' incised, on the other side three hounds following a scent across open fields.

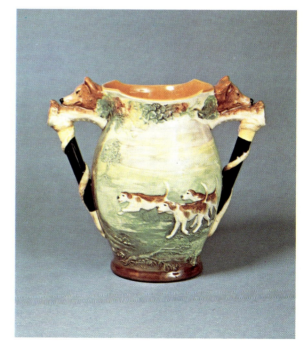

The Apothecary Loving-Cup

Limited edition of 600
Date issued: 1934
Height: 6 in
Signed: NOKE & H FENTON

The supplier of love-potions and poisons as well as medicinal drugs, the apothecary played an important role in Elizabethan times. If his potions were held to be particularly powerful he could become a wealthy man – although it was best not to ask what went into them! Romeo, hearing that Juliet is dead, remembers an apothecary from whom he can buy poison for himself:

In tattered weeds with overwhelming brows
Culling of simples; meagre were his looks;
And in his needy shop a tortoise hung
An alligator stuff'd and other skins
Of ill-shaped fishes.

The apothecary depicted on the loving-cup is a successful man: he is seen talking to a richly dressed lady while two dandies wait in an ante-chamber as another customer is admitted by a page. There are pots of ingredients, a pestle and mortar and a large globe. Skeletons adorn the walls and the ghostly faces of lovers are moulded in relief around the rim and on the handles. On the base are the words spoken by Romeo before he takes his poison 'O true apothecary Thy drugs are quick'.

The Wandering Minstrel Loving-Cup

Limited edition of 600
Date issued: 1934
Height: $5\frac{1}{2}$ in
Signed: NOKE & FENTON

In mediaeval England wandering minstrels were a popular source of entertainment, recounting the latest events in ballad form as well as singing old favourites. In legend Richard Lionheart's minstrel, Blondel, travelled all over Europe looking for his master, secretly imprisoned by the Duke of Austria. Coming to a castle with one solitary prisoner he sang the first half of a song which Richard had helped him compose. When the prisoner finished the tune he knew it was Richard and returned to England with his news.

This minstrel, sitting footsore on a wall with his lute and meagre possessions, barked at by a dog, must have been pleased to see the lady of the castle appear with a page carrying refreshments. On the base is the phrase 'a merryman moping mum' from a ballad sung by Jack Point in Gilbert and Sullivan's operetta 'Yeomen of the Guard'.

It's the song of a merryman moping mum,
Whose soul was sad, and whose glance was glum,
Who supped no sup, and who craved no crumb,
As he sighed for the love of a ladye.

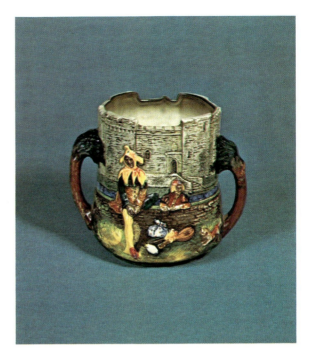

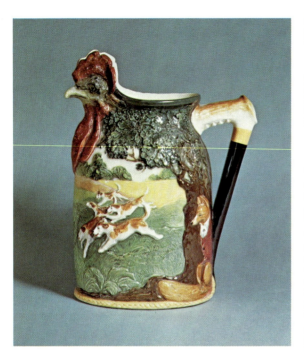

Master of Foxhounds Presentation Jug

Limited edition of 500
Date issued: 1930
Height: 13 in
Signed: NOKE

There can be few more English sights than to watch hounds in full cry followed by the huntsmen in their pink with the field galloping behind. Fox-hunting has been popular in England since the 18th century as, unlike shooting, it was not a restricted sport and anyone could and did join in. With the spreading of enclosures and the growth of hedgerows and walls dividing up the fields jumping became common and the centuries-old European style of collected riding gave way in England to one based on the dash and free movement required on the hunting field. The tasks of the Master himself are varied, ranging from hunting two to three times a week during the season to maintaining goodwill amongst the local farmers and landowners and controlling the riders of the Hunt. He is helped by a Huntsman and one or two whippers-in who help control the pack. The hounds themselves (never called dogs) are paired off into couples and the size of the pack is given in couples.

The oval-shaped jug, with its lip modelled as a rooster's head, shows a pack of hounds running across a field hunting for the fox who sits under a tree, dressed in Pink, calmly watching the chase. The handle is in the form of a whip with the thong trailing around the base. This jug is commonly known as the MFH jug.

Regency Coach Jug

Limited edition of 500
Date issued: 1931
Height: 10 in
Signed: NOKE

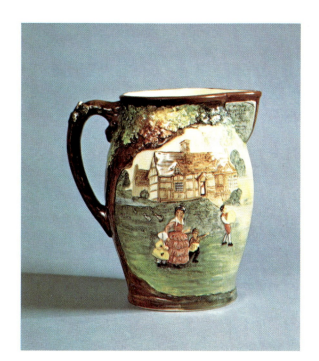

Before the railways were built, coaching was the only means of travelling across the country and by the time of the Regency (1811–20) great advances had been made. Competing lines, changing horses at the great coaching inns, raced each other to prove that they provided the fastest service. Journeys were uncomfortable with many having to travel on top whatever the weather and there was the added danger of highwaymen. The coachmen with their many-tiered coats and yard-long horns were idolised by young boys and commanded great respect. The roads themselves gradually improved with the innovations introduced of Telford and MacAdam but in 1817 it still took 36 hours to cover the 186 miles from Manchester to London.

The jug shows a large manor house with the lady of the manor and her two children on the spacious lawns watching as a coach draws up before an inn. Under a tree lies a rustic with his pint of ale. The lip has a parchment inscribed 'Regency Coach London to Brighton Monday IX o'clock' and an inn sign for 'Ye Olde Inn'. Brighton, only 55 miles from London, became a popular summer resort when the Prince Regent (the future George IV) built a summer residence there.

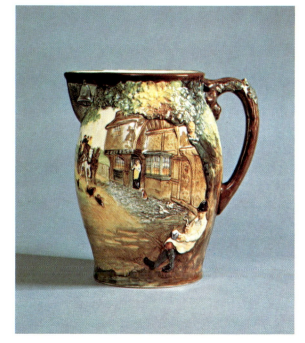

Treasure Island Jug

Limited edition of 600
Date issued: 1934
Height: $7\frac{1}{2}$ in
Signed: NOKE & FENTON

First appearing as a serial in 1881 under the title 'The Sea Cook or Treasure Island', this is the novel that established Robert Louis Stevenson as a leading fiction writer. The tale is told through the eyes of Jim Hawkins, a young lad whose mother runs the 'Admiral Benbow', a tavern in the West Country. When an old buccaneer comes to stay the inn is invaded by his former comrades led by the blind pirate Pew, searching for the map of Captain Flint's buried treasure which the old man has hidden. Jim outwits them and escapes with the chart to Squire Trelawney who sets sail for Treasure Island with his friend Dr Livesay and Jim on the schooner 'Hispaniola'. Unknown to them many of the crew are pirates recruited by the cook, the one-legged Long John Silver, who plans to seize the ship and the treasure. The plot is discovered by Jim and after a series of adventures the buccaneers are overcome with the aid of Ben Gunn, a marooned pirate.

Depicted on the jug are two pirates burying the treasure-chest, their long-boat drawn up on the beach and their ship waiting off-shore, while on the other side Long John Silver (with his parrot), Jim and some of the crew try to find the treasure from the map. A sketch of the chart appears on the base.

Robin Hood Loving-Cup

Limited edition of 600
Date issued: 1938
Height: 8½ in
Signed: NOKE & H FENTON

Robin Hood, who traditionally robbed the rich to give to the poor, is undoubtedly one of the best known of English characters. For many years attempts have been made to prove his existence, but the issue is confused by the number of places claiming to be the scene of his escapades. Some have documentary evidence to back their claim; for example in the Pipe Roll of 1230 for York there is a 'Robertus Hood fugitivus'. The first detailed history 'lytell Geste of Robyn Hoode' c 1495 places him in Yorkshire but later he is moved to Sherwood Forest in Nottinghamshire, finally being made Earl of Huntingdon. Of the many ballads and plays in which he appears, one of the best known is 'Robin Hood and Guy of Gisborne', which tells how the giant, Little John, is captured by the Sheriff of Nottingham and tied to a tree. Meanwhile Robin meets and slays Guy of Gisborne and takes his clothes and arms. The Sheriff mistakes him for Guy and gives him permission to kill Little John but instead he turns him loose and the Sheriff and company flee.

Various members of the Merry Men are shown on the loving-cup: Friar Tuck, Maid Marion and Little John under the oak trees, and Robin drawing his bow watched by Will Scarlet, Friar Tuck and Little John. The names of those in the first group are incised on the handle to their right.

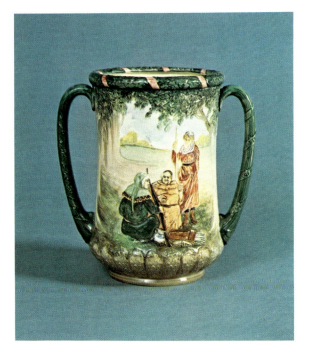

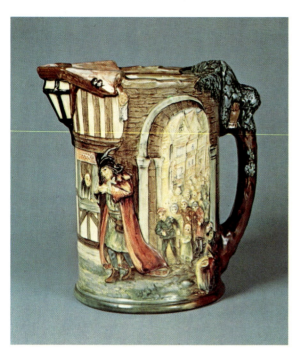

Pied Piper Jug

Limited edition of 600
Date issued: 1934
Height: 10 in
Signed: NOKE & H FENTON

First included in 'Dramatic Romances', 1845, the Pied Piper of Hamelin was written while Robert Browning was still relatively unknown outside literary circles. The poem tells the tale of the town of Hamelin in Brunswick (Germany) which is overrun by a plague of rats. In desperation the townspeople descend on the mayor demanding a solution when

'... in did come the strangest figure!
His queer long coat from heel to head
Was half of yellow and half of red'

The piper offers to rid the town of rats for 1,000 guilders which is eagerly accepted. Playing strange music on his pipe he leads the rats to the river Weser where they drown. He returns for his reward but is only offered 50 guilders. Enraged he plays again and now the children follow him to a hill called Koppenburg where a door opens and they all disappear inside.
    Both facets of the tale are illustrated on the jug, with the mayor and council watching the rats depart on one side and the piper leading the children through the streets on the other. A version of the story is recorded on the base.

The Three Musketeers Loving-Cup

Limited edition of 600
Date issued: 1936
Height: 10 in
Signed: NOKE & H FENTON

Alexander Dumas' most famous novel, 'The Three Musketeers', tells of the adventures of the impetuous d'Artagnan and his three companions, the quiet and wise Athos, strong and simple Porthos and secretive Aramis – the musketeers of Louis XIII of France. The story centres around the love of Queen Anne of France for the English Duke of Buckingham and the efforts of Cardinal Richelieu, the king's chief minister, to expose her. He is aided by the infamous Miladi – who plans the Duke's assassination – and the Chevalier Rochefort but is foiled by the efforts of the four friends to protect the queen. In the sequels, 'Twenty Years After' and 'The Vicomte de Bragelonne' (which included the Man in the Iron Mask sequence) the four are followed through maturity to death.

The principal characters are illustrated on the cup – on one side the three musketeers stand in front of a church, on the other, a street scene, they stand to the rear with d'Artagnan, watching the Cardinal and Rochefort (to the right). The handles, modelled as the trophies of war and the accoutrements of pleasure, display the love of an active vigorous life which is portrayed so well in Dumas' works.

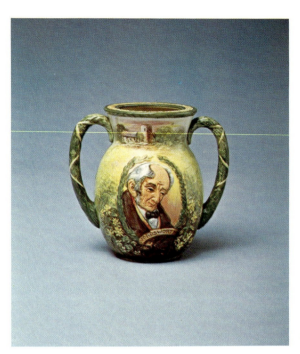

William Wordsworth Loving-Cup

Unlimited edition
Date issued: 1933
Height: 6½ in
Signed: NOKE

William Wordsworth (1770–1850) is today remembered as the author of some of the most beautiful poetry in the English language. He was born in Cockermouth, Cumbria, and grew to love the Lake District, returning to live at Grasmere in 1799. At first he lived with his sister Dorothy in Dove Cottage (now a museum), then moved to Rydal Mount. Sir Henry Doulton, a great admirer of his works, never forgot his meeting with the poet, calling him '... the most potent force in the poetry of the nineteenth century'. Noke shared Sir Henry's regard for Wordsworth and produced this loving-cup to commemorate his being made Poet Laureate in 1843.

The cup illustrates one of the best-known poems:

I wandered lonely as a cloud
That floats on high o'er vales and hills,
When all at once I saw a crowd,
A host, of golden daffodils;
Beside the lake, beneath the trees,
Fluttering and dancing in the breeze.

On one side is a portrait of Wordsworth below Grasmere Church where he lies buried, on the other is Dorothy among a mass of daffodils below Dove Cottage.

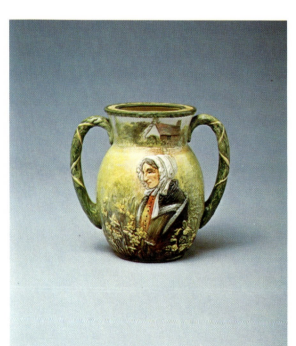

William Shakespeare Jug

Limited edition of 1,000
Date issued: 1933
Height: 10¾ in
Signed: NOKE

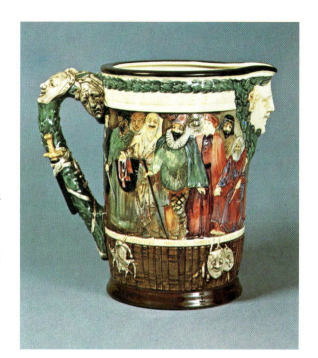

William Shakespeare (1546–1616) was born in Stratford-on-Avon, the son of a respected husbandman and educated at a free grammar school. He married Anne Hathaway in 1582 and a few years later moved to London where he probably started work in one of the two theatres. Soon he was writing as well as acting, his name appearing in the cast-lists until 1603. His plays were very popular at the time and it is said that he wrote 'The Merry Wives of Windsor' at the request of Queen Elizabeth I. Shakespeare became wealthy from his stagework, purchasing New Place, the largest house in Stratford, in 1597; by the time he retired there in 1610 he had built up a considerable estate. He was buried in Stratford Church where one of his few authentic portraits, a monument with a bust, can still be seen.

The jug features some of his best-known characters in full-length relief, given here from left to right: Hamlet, Othello, Autolycus (The Winter's Tale), Portia (The Merchant of Venice), Macbeth, King Lear (seated), Ophelia (Hamlet), Shylock (Merchant of Venice), Touchstone (As You Like It), Katherine (Taming of the Shrew), Falstaff (Henry IV & Merry Wives). Written around the rim is GREAT HEIR OF FAME DEAR SON OF MEMORY; the handle shows the masks of tragedy and comedy with volumes of his plays; more masks and jester's accoutrements are moulded around the base.

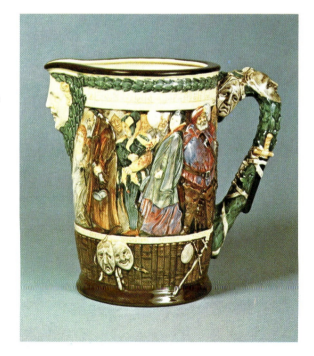

Guy Fawkes Jug

Limited edition of 600
Date issued: 1934
Height: $7\frac{1}{2}$ in
Signed: FENTON

A few days before the state opening of Parliament on November 5th 1605, a letter was delivered to the King, James I, warning him not to attend. It was then discovered that one Thomas Percy had sub-let a cellar underneath Parliament House and bought a stock of coal from the landlady. On the eve of the opening Sir Thomas Knyvet, a privy councillor and Justice of the Peace for Westminster, searched the cellar and found Guy Fawkes standing guard over an enormous pile of gunpowder, iron bars, coal and wood. Under torture he revealed the names of the other conspirators including the leader Robert Catesby, who was killed resisting arrest. The incident was widely assumed to be a Catholic plot but there is evidence that an agent provocateur encouraged the attempt in order to create hostility towards them and the Jesuits in particular. The event is celebrated throughout Britain by the symbolic burning of Guy Fawkes on November 5th.

The jug portrays Sir Thomas Knyvet standing at the base of the cellar steps with drawn sword surprising Guy Fawkes by the barrels of gunpowder. More guards can be seen running to aid Sir Thomas. The handle is modelled as a flaming torch and on the base is written the order of execution of Guy Fawkes signed by James.

Tower of London Jug

Limited edition of 500
Date issued: 1933
Height: $9\frac{1}{2}$ in
Signed: NOKE & H FENTON

Originally built as a fortress to defend London, then royal residence, state prison and now an arsenal, The Tower of London was founded by William the Conqueror (1078) and greatly enlarged by Henry III in the 13th century, the outer curtain and moat being finished by Edward I. Among the prisoners held were King David of Scotland (1346–57), King John of France (1356–60), Princess Elizabeth and Sir Walter Raleigh (1605–6). The Tower was also a place of execution: Anne Boleyn both married Henry VIII, and was beheaded within its walls.

Today the Tower is visited by thousands every year as within are kept the Crown Jewels guarded by the Yeomen of the Guard (or Beefeaters). The Yeomen are chosen from time-expired Warrant Officers and NCOs and still dress in costumes dating from the time of Edward VI. The Tower is also home to a flock of ravens, and according to legend when they leave, England will fall.

The jug portrays two groups: a lord and lady attended by Yeomen before Traitors Gate and Jack Point (who features in the operetta 'Yeomen of the Guard') and a turnkey with more guards. A shield with the lions of England forms the spout and the handle is decorated with axes, pikes, chains and a suit of armour.

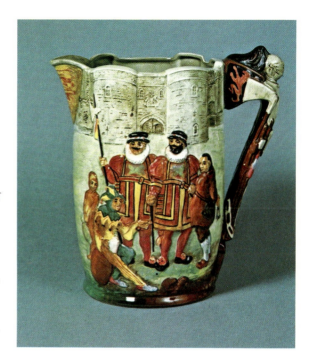

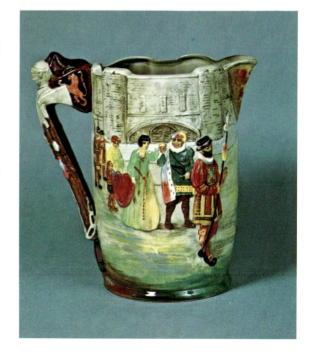

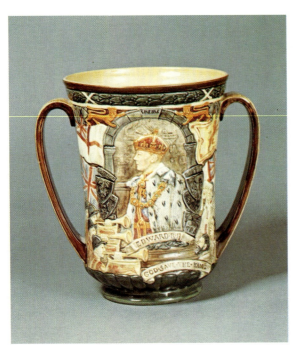

King Edward VIII Coronation Loving-Cup (large)

Limited edition of 2000 of which 1080 were sold
Date issued: 1937
Height: 10 in
Signed: NOKE & FENTON

The king who was never crowned, Edward VIII, was born on June 23rd 1894 at the White Lodge, Richmond and christened Edward Albert Christopher George Andrew Patrick David. He became a naval cadet at an early age and during the Great War he held a commission in the Grenadier Guards and saw action at the front. He was a popular Prince of Wales and was highly acclaimed on the many overseas tours he undertook. When his father died in January 1936, Edward saw his duty 'to modernize the monarchy within its traditional glory and strength' but decided to abdicate before the coronation after a reign of only 325 days. In his farewell broadcast he said '. . . I have found it impossible to carry the heavy responsibility and to discharge my duties without the help and support of the woman I love.' Created Duke of Windsor he entered a self-imposed exile in France with Wallis Simpson, the American divorcee he now married.

Edward is portrayed in a half-length portrait wearing his coronation regalia, surrounded by flags representing the United Kingdom, Scotland and the Royal Navy. Below are trumpeters and representatives of the public with the inscription 'EDWARD VIII GOD SAVE THE KING'. The reverse shows St George before Windsor Castle among heraldic devices and Commonwealth flags. Incised on the handles are the names of various Commonwealth countries: Australia, Canada, India, New Zealand, South Africa, Jamaica, Trinidad, Barbados, Ceylon, Kenya and the State of Tasmania.

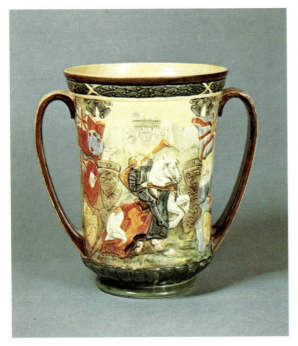

King Edward VIII Coronation Loving-Cup (small)

Limited edition of 1000 of which 454 were sold
Date issued: 1937
Height: 6½ in
Signed: NOKE

This small loving-cup was also made to commemorate the accession of Edward VIII but is much less elaborate in design than the larger version. On one side is a frontal portrait of Edward as Prince of Wales with the Prince's personal insignia of three ostrich feathers to either side with flags representing Scotland, Ireland, Australia and New Zealand. Below are incised Tudor roses, thistles and shamrocks, the national emblems of, respectively, England, Scotland and Ireland together with a shield bearing the Royal Arms. On the reverse is a profile of the king in coronation regalia above the legend 'GOD SAVE THE KING' The Union Jack and the White Ensign are to either side. Incised on the cup are the names of various Commonwealth countries and provinces: Jamaica, New South Wales, Kenya, Crown Colony Ceylon, Natal, South Africa, Canada, Australia, India and Quebec.

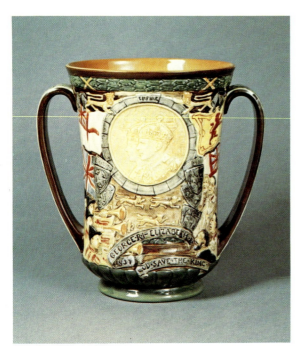

King George VI and Queen Elizabeth Coronation Loving-Cup (large)

Limited edition of 2000
Date issued: 1937
Height: 10½ in
Signed: NOKE & H FENTON

Albert Frederick Arthur George, known as Bertie, was born on December 14th 1895, the second son of the future George V. Like his brother he became a naval cadet and later, as a sub-lieutenant he showed sufficient 'coolness and courage' during the Battle of Jutland to be mentioned in despatches. After the war he became interested in industrial affairs at Trinity College, Cambridge, earning the nick-name 'Foreman'. Then he met Elizabeth Bowes-Lyon and courted her for several years before their marriage at Westminster Abbey in 1923. Three years later their first child Elizabeth was born, followed by Margaret in 1930.

When his elder brother, Edward VIII, decided to abdicate, Bertie took his father's name and held to the original coronation date in order to make the transition as smooth as possible. George always had good relations with the post-war Labour government and earned the title 'The People's King'. He died after a long illness on October 6th 1952.

Due to the suddenness of his accession this loving-cup is very similar to that of Edward VIII. The main difference is that the King and Queen are shown in profile within a portrait medallion with the legends 'GEORGE R I-ELIZABETH R 1937' and 'GOD SAVE THE KING' below.

King George VI and Queen Elizabeth Coronation Loving-Cup (small)

Limited edition of 2000
Date issued: 1937
Height: 6½ in
Signed: NOKE & FENTON

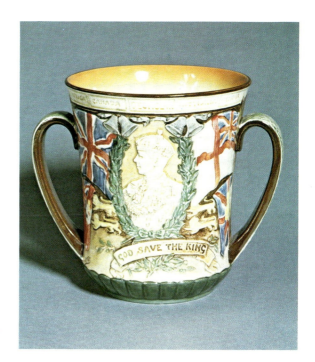

This small loving-cup features a profile of George VI in coronation regalia with the legend 'GOD SAVE THE KING' below. To either side are flags representing the United Kingdom and the Royal Navy. On the reverse is a profile of the Queen, also in coronation regalia, with the legend 'ELIZABETH R' below. To her left is the flag of St Andrew, Patron Saint of Scotland, with the Scottish lion to the right. Impressed below are thistles, shamrocks and roses. Around the rim, above the King and Queen respectively, are impressed S AFRICA CANADA GEORGE R I AUSTRALIA INDIA and S AFRICA AUSTRALIA OUR QUEEN CANADA N ZEALAND.

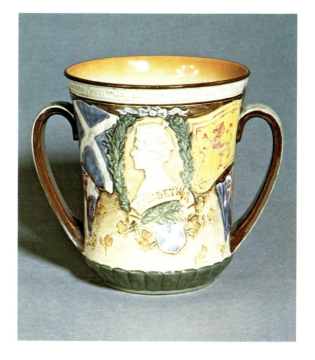

King George V and Queen Mary Silver Jubilee Loving-Cup

Limited edition of 1000
Date issued: 1935
Height: 10 in
Signed: NOKE & FENTON

As second son, George Frederick Ernest Albert (1865–1935) did not expect to rule, but following the death of his elder brother in 1892 he became Duke of York (second in line to the throne) and a year later married his brother's former fiancée Princess May of Teck (1867–1953). As Prince of Wales (1901–10) he travelled extensively, his itineraries including Canada, Australia and India. On his accession to the throne in 1910 May took the name Mary and proved a loyal support for the next 26 years. During the Great War George changed the name of the Royal house from Saxe-Coburg-Gotha to Windsor because of the prevalent anti-German feeling. Overseas, his reign saw the start of the long transition from Empire to Commonwealth.

This, the first Royal limited edition loving-cup, has a portrait medallion in profile of the King and Queen crowned, surrounded by the flags of the United Kingdom, Scotland and the Royal Navy. Below are Commonwealth representatives and trumpeters and above is 'HAPPY AND GLORIOUS'. The reverse shows St George (as designed for Doulton by Stanley Thorogood) before Windsor Castle. On the handles are the names of various Commonwealth provinces and countries: Jamaica, Crown Colony of India, Kenya, South Africa, New South Wales, Canada, Australia, Natal, New Zealand, Ceylon and Quebec. Around the rim are laurel leaves interspersed with the dates 1910 and 1935. A version with the King and Queen uncrowned has also been recorded.

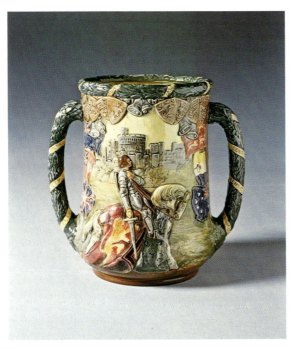

Queen Elizabeth II Coronation Loving-Cup

Limited edition of 1,000
Date issued: 1953
Height: 10½ in
Signed: NOKE & FENTON

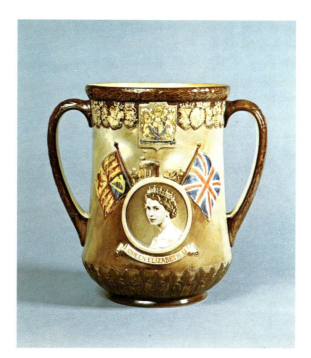

Queen Elizabeth II was born on April 21st 1926, daughter of the then Duke and Duchess of York. Her full name is Elizabeth Alexandra Mary but she was known to her family as Lilibet. She married Philip Mountbatten on November 20th 1947 and they have four children – Charles, Prince of Wales, Anne, Andrew and Edward. On her father's death, on February 6th 1952, she became Queen and was crowned a year later.

The Queen's portrait in relief is surmounted by the Union Jack and the Royal Standard. The latter displays the three lions of England, the Scottish lion and the Irish harp. Wales is not represented as it is a principality not a kingdom. Above are the full Royal Arms, with the golden lion (England) and silver unicorn (Scotland). The Garter (established c1344) encircles the shield with its motto 'Honi soit qui mal y pense'. The lion crest was first worn by Richard Lionheart and 'Dieu et mon droit' has been the sovereign's motto since the days of Henry VI.

The present Queen's famous namesake, Elizabeth I is remembered on the reverse, with her portrait shown against a backdrop of three galleons illustrating the ascendance of England as a great naval power. Various shields are moulded around the top rim of the cup.

Queen Elizabeth II Coronation Jug

Although not a limited edition, this small (6¼ in) jug closely resembles the larger version. On one side is a photographic portrait of the Queen with the Union Jack and the Royal Standard to either side. Below is the legend 'ELIZABETH R'. The reverse has a relief view of Windsor Castle. A frieze of shields decorates the top, with a Tudor rose above the medallion portrait. Issued in 1953, it is unsigned.

Queen Elizabeth II Silver Jubilee Loving-Cup

Limited edition of 250
Date issued: 1977
Height: $10\frac{1}{2}$ in
Signed: REG JOHNSON

The Silver Jubilee was widely celebrated throughout the United Kingdom with street parties in every town and village, and particular attention being paid to children. During 1977 the Queen toured extensively and received a rapturous welcome wherever she went. The popularity of the monarch is in part due to her efforts to become closer to the people: by sending her children to school; by televising her Christmas broadcasts and by allowing a detailed film to be made of her day-to-day life which showed facets of both her Royal duties and her private life that had never before been seen.

The richly coloured loving-cup features the Queen in profile in her coronation robes above shields representing Scotland, England and Wales with the Union Jack, the White Ensign, the Blue Ensign and the Scottish lion to the sides. She is attended by various countrymen including a Yeoman of the Guard and the Royal Trumpeters. Below is the legend 'ELIZABETH II SILVER JUBILEE'. The reverse displays the Royal Coat of Arms with the motto 'DIEU ET MON DROIT'. The names of all the Commonwealth countries are incised either on or beneath the handles with their modelled lions' heads.